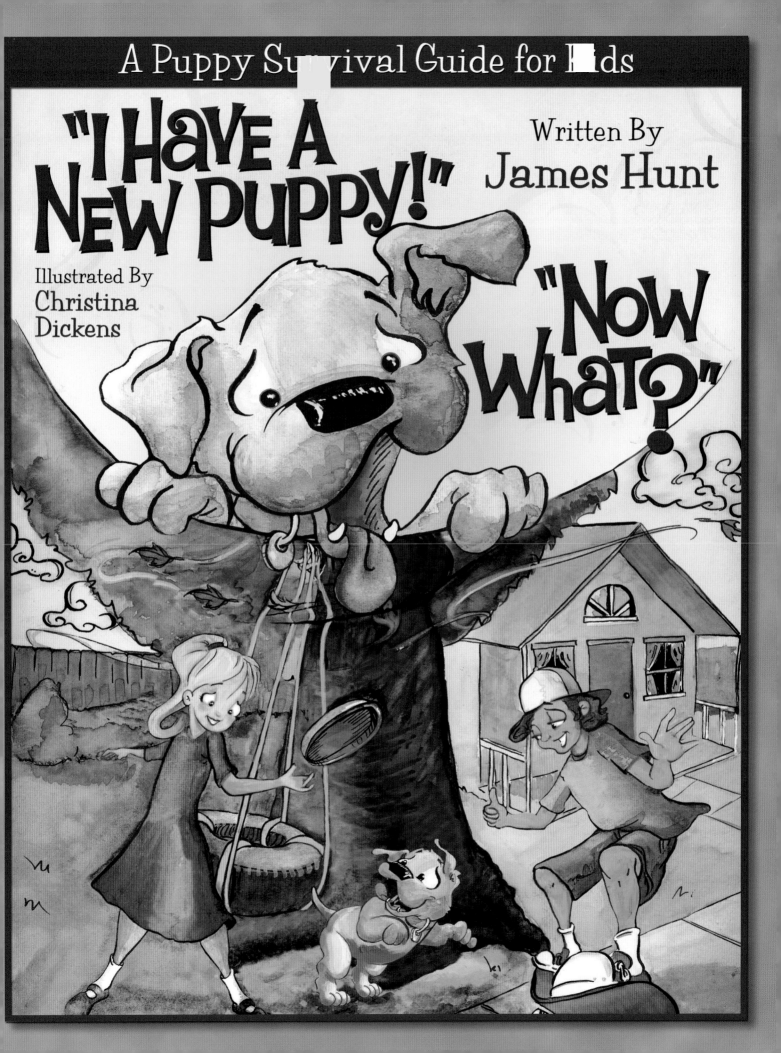

Dedication

I would like to dedicate this book to my two beautiful
children, Noah and Nicole, and to my loving wife,
Anna, who makes the sun rise and set for all of us.

In loving memory of the best friend
I've ever had—my dog, Bear.

—*James Hunt*

Text copyright © 2005 by James L. Hunt
Illustrations © 2007 by Christina Dickens

All rights reserved. Published by J.L. Hunt Publishing Company.

No part of this publication may be reproduced, stored in a retrieval system, or transmitted in any form or by
any means, electronic, mechanical, photocopying, recording, or otherwise, without permission of the publisher.

For information regarding permission, write to:
J.L. Hunt Publishing Company
Atten: Permissions Department
27881 La Paz Road, Suite G-124
Laguna Niguel, CA 92677

www.jlhuntpublishing.com

Library of Congress Cataloging-in-Publication Data available.
ISBN: 978-0-9769401-0-4
10 9 8 7 6 5 4 3 2 1   07 08 09 10 11
Printed in USA
First Edition, May, 2007

It was a beautiful Spring day, the birds were singing and the flowers were blooming.

But all was not well at Niki and Noah's house.

They finally got the puppy they always dreamed of. But soon they realized having a puppy wasn't all fun and games. They were becoming aware that a puppy doesn't magically grow into a well-behaved, obedient dog overnight.

But for Niki and Noah, something magical did happen...

POOF!

Suddenly a cloud of white smoke appeared. As the smoke faded, the children saw a friendly fireman and his dog standing right in front of them!

"Wow!" exclaimed Niki excitedly.

"Check that out!" Noah said. They couldn't believe their eyes.

"Hi, kids" The Fireman said. "I'm Fireman James and this is my dog, Flame. We're responding to a "P.A." in this area."

"P.A.?" asked Noah, scratching his head. "What's a P.A.?"

"A puppy alert," Fireman James responded.

Niki looked confused. "We didn't send a puppy alert."

"Sure you did," Fireman James explained. "Flame and I both magically knew that you two and your puppy needed help."

Suddenly another strange thing happened. The kids heard the coolest voice ever. Flame, Fireman James' faithful companion began to talk!

"I can sniff out an unhappy family miles away," said Flame as he put his nose in the air and took a good, long whiff.

Noah was so excited. "Awesome! You can talk!" he said as he stared at Flame in amazement.

As Flame looked around their yard, he saw all the damage their new little puppy had caused. He joked to Fireman James, "Looks like we need a clean-up on aisle three!"

Niki couldn't believe her eyes or her ears. She wished some of her friends were around to see them. Would they ever believe her? In a surprised voice she said, "I've never seen a talking Dalmatian with red spots before!"

Fireman James chuckled at their amazement. This happened every time Flame was introduced to a new family. "Flame is a one-of-a kind Super Dog," he said.

Flame started to blush. He always got embarrassed when someone gave him a compliment. He said shyly, "Well dude, I don't know about 'Super'..."

Niki couldn't help herself and started to laugh. "Look," she giggled, "his cheeks are getting red too. Flame's cheeks are getting as red as his spots!"

Fireman James asked the kids, "So why the sad faces?" He had seen this before. When a family gets a new puppy, they aren't always as prepared as they think they are. He knew he and Flame could help.

Noah couldn't wait to help explain their situation. "Our new puppy, Bear, chews everything. He tore up my baseball glove and chewed on my skateboard. He thinks my hands and feet are chew toys and that doesn't feel so great! Can you believe that?"

Niki wanted to add her side to the story. "Bear jumps and barks and goes potty everywhere. Our mom and dad get so upset, but it's really not our fault. After all, he's just a puppy. What do you think we should do?"

"Looks like we have a Code-Red Puppy Alert," Fireman James said as he glanced over at Flame. "Flame and I have seen this a thousand times. I think your family is a little confused about what Bear needs."

Noah and Niki thought about all they had done for Bear.

Noah said, "But we make sure he has food and water and we give him snacks."

"And we give him lots of love and pet him all the time," added Niki.

Bear barked and wagged his tail. He wanted everyone to know how much he enjoyed it when the kids scratched behind his ears and rubbed his belly.

Flame understood Bear's bark. "Those are all great things, but a puppy needs more. I should know. If Fireman James hadn't given me all the care and training I needed as a puppy, I wouldn't be the cool dog I am today."

Fireman James smiled at
Flame. "Flame has made my
life incredible by becoming a
Super Dog." Niki was dying to ask
Fireman James a question. "Where *did* you get Flame?"

Fireman James sat down on the stoop next to the kids and
began his magical tale. "Kids, let me tell you the story of the
day I met Flame."

"It was just a typical day at the fire station when my crew and I received a call to respond to a fire at an old abandoned warehouse. When we arrived, the building was already in flames.

When we went in to attack the fire, we found a Dalmatian and her puppies trapped inside.

My crew grabbed the mother and her puppies and rushed out. I stayed behind to make sure everyone got out safely.

Just as I was leaving, I saw one of the puppies behind a box and went to scoop him up, when—**BAM!** Part of the roof collapsed. If I hadn't turned back for the puppy, I would have been crushed.

But I wasn't out of danger yet, the front exit was *blocked!*

I ran for the rear exit when more of the roof started to fall. I had to act fast. This building used to be a magic supply warehouse. In the corner was a tall metal box, the kind magicians use to make people disappear. I jumped into the box to avoid the burning beams, but the beams slammed the door shut and trapped the puppy and I inside.

All I could think of was getting out fast and to a safe place—when all of a sudden—WE DISAPPEARED!

When I finally opened the box, we were back at the fire station! I couldn't believe it. What an adventure!

I tried to use the Magic Box again, but it didn't work. It worked only when Flame and I were inside.

That's when I knew there was something magical about this puppy."

Fireman James continued his story, "I decided to name him 'Flame' because his spots grew in red instead of black!"

"I raised and trained him to be a special rescue dog. My crew and I turned the station into a Dog Emergency Station."

"I was using the Magic Box to get to emergencies, but Flame was getting too big to fit inside, so I modified my fire engine with the Magic Box. Now all Flame and I have to do is get in and push the magic button and we are off to our next adventure!"

"I have the most incredible life with Fireman James," Flame added, scratching his belly.

"We get to meet wonderful new families just like yours all the time, and I especially like to make new dog friends," Flame said as he barked happily at Bear.

The kids really enjoyed hearing Fireman James' magical story. "Wow! That was great," said Noah. "Can we go on an adventure too?" asked Niki. "Sure!" Fireman James answered.

Then Fireman James asked Noah and Niki, "How would you like to be E.P.T.'s?"

"What's an E.P.T.?" Noah asked.

"An Expert Puppy Trainer," Fireman James explained.

Noah and Niki were excited, they both asked at the same time, "Can we be E.P.T.'s?"

Fireman James was thrilled to see their enthusiasm, he knew that becoming Expert Puppy Trainers was just what the kids needed to help Bear become a trusted, well behaved puppy.

"First, you have to take the E.P.T. trainee pledge. You have to learn the three 'P's'—you have to promise to be **P**repared, have **P**atience, and have **PF**un! explained Fireman James.

Being very good at spelling, Niki knew there was something wrong with that pledge. "Hey—wait a minute!"she said, "Fun doesn't start with a P!"

Fireman James laughed. "That's right, Niki, it's up to you to put the "fun" into puppy training!"

Bear was so excited the kids were becoming E.P.T.'s, that he began to bark and run in a circle.

3 P'S
Prepared
Patience
Pfun

Fireman James knew now was a great time to begin. "Looks like someone is ready to start his training." Flame chuckled, "I think this 'little dude' needs to go potty!"

"Terrific!" exclaimed Fireman James. "Potty training is a great place to start your E.P.T. training. Where is Bear's special potty spot?"

Niki laughed, *"Everywhere* is his special spot, that's the problem!"

"Well, Bear needs to have one specific place where he can go potty," explained Fireman James.

"Now, here's a fun way to get started. Gather the whole family together and take a walk outside and decide exactly where Bear's special potty place will be."

"Everyone should pick a phrase to use when telling Bear it's time to go potty. The phrase could be 'go potty', 'get busy', or 'do your business'. Pick any phrase, but everyone needs to agree on using the same one. You'll confuse Bear if everyone uses a different phrase."

Flame couldn't wait to tell the kids his 'potty phrase,' "Fireman James used 'go poof, poof' when I was a puppy. That did the trick for me!"

"Ruff, ruff," barked Bear, as he ran in a circle.

Winking at Bear, Flame said, "Bear likes that one."

"Come on 'little dude,' I'll show you where to go 'poof, poof.' Once you know your 'potty phrase' you'll have no problem understanding what your owners want you to do."

The two dogs ran off to Bear's special spot.

Following Flame and Bear to his special potty spot, Niki thought of an important question. "How do we stop Bear from going potty when he is inside the house?"

Fireman James was quick to answer, "Never let him out of your sight. He may wander off looking for his special 'potty spot,' when he doesn't find it, he'll go where he shouldn't. Bear should always be in one of three places: with you, outside in his potty place or in his crate."

"What's a crate?" Noah asked curiously.

Fireman James was happy to explain, "A crate is a wonderful thing for your puppy. A crate is your puppy's little house."

"I love my crate," smiled Flame. "It's where I sleep and feel safe. The only place I like better is my dog run."

"What's a dog run?" Niki wondered.

Flame got excited. He asked the kids and Bear, "Would you like to go see my dog run?"

Fireman James leaned down to pat his faithful sidekick. "Great idea, Flame!" "Come on kids, let's get started on our exciting adventure!"

POOF!

In no time at all, the gang arrived at the fire station. Noah and Niki couldn't believe they had just ridden on a Magical Fire Truck.

Fireman James climbed out of the vehicle. "Welcome to Station 111. This is where it all happened. Over there is Flame's dog run; A dog run is a special place outside where your puppy can play, sleep and eat. It's also a place where your puppy can stay out of trouble."

Flame laughed, "I wasn't always a 'Super Dog.' I was a very unruly puppy. Fireman James helped me learn the right way to behave and my dog run saved me from getting into a whole lot of trouble!"

The kids and Bear really enjoyed the fire station. As Noah looked around he noticed something, "Hey! Where does this pole go?" he asked.

Flame was quick to answer. "That's the crew's quarters and where I keep my crate, would you like to see it?"

Bear barked enthusiastically as Noah and Niki excitedly said, "Wow!" "That would be great!"

Fireman James looked serious. "It's a special place, not everyone gets to go up there, but since you are E.P.T. trainees, I think maybe we can make an exception."

27

The gang was magically whisked upstairs to the crew's quarters.

"Here we are!" Fireman James exclaimed. "Here's Flame's special crate and the crew's quarters. When you complete your E.P.T. training, you'll get a badge like this."

He held up a shiny silver badge. Excited at the sight of the silver badge, Noah quickly asked, "When do we start our training?"

"You already have," laughed Fireman James. "So far you've learned how to potty train Bear, you've learned about dog crates and dog runs."

"Wow," exclaimed Niki.
"We've been having so much fun,
we didn't even notice that we were learning."

Noah heard a strange noise. "Oh no!" he cried.

"We've been so busy having fun, we didn't notice Bear chewing on Fireman James' gear!"

"Not to worry," laughed Fireman James. "It's natural for a puppy to chew. It's what they do best! But, you must train Bear to only chew on his own toys."

"How do we do that?" asked Noah.

"Simple, use an easy E.P.T. technique called 'Tug-And-A-No,'" Fireman James said. "When Bear starts chewing on something that he shouldn't, simply "tug" on his leash and firmly say 'NO!' Then, quickly replace one of his own toys with the object he was chewing upon and then tell him *'Good Boy!'*"

Flame grabbed a rubber fire hydrant. "Bear can have one of my toys if you want to show how a 'Tug-And-A-No' works."

"That's a great idea," Fireman James said as he took the toy from Flame.

As the children watched carefully, Fireman James showed them how "Tug-And-A-No" worked.

Noah asked, "Can I use a 'Tug-And-A-No' when Bear grabs my hand? His teeth are *really* sharp!"

"Absolutely!" Fireman James answered. "When Bear grabs you by the hands or feet this is called 'Mouthing.' You must show Bear that hands and feet are not chew toys."

Now, the kids were really getting into their E.P.T. training.

"What about when he jumps on people?" Niki asked.

Fireman James responded, "When Bear jumps give him a 'Tug-And-A-No' and immediately follow by giving him a 'Quiet Five.'

"A 'Quiet Five'? What's that?" Niki asked.

"It's like a time-out," Fireman James answered. "You ignore Bear and count to five, but, remember—you always want to praise good behavior and ignore bad behavior."

Bear loved his new toy. "Ruff, ruff!" barked the happy puppy.

Flame patted Bear's head. "Bear was thanking me for his new chew toy. It's totally cool, 'dude.'"

Fireman James asked, "So, who wants to slide down the fire pole?"

"I do!" exclaimed Noah.

Just then, Niki turned to look at Bear. "Wait! Bear is scared," she cried.

Flame walked over to Bear and put his arm around him. "It's okay 'little dude,' I'll show you how to do it. Ride it like a wave!"

Afterwards, as Fireman James
walked everyone back to the Magical
Fire Engine, he explained, "It's important
to expose Bear to *all* kinds of things so
he won't be afraid of anything." This is
called *Socializing*.

"So now that will be our next adventure!"

POOF!

It was a beautiful afternoon when Fireman James and his gang arrived at the park. The park was buzzing with all kinds of bustling activity.

Noah asked, "Why are we at the park, Fireman James?"

"Good question, Noah." Fireman James continued. "We are here to introduce Bear to the real world! It's what we call 'Socialization.' You need to show Bear that his world is a friendly and safe place."

"Remember the fire pole? At first Bear was afraid, but once he realized it was okay, he had such fun!"

Noah knew he was on to something. "I get it!" he said. "We need to show Bear different people, places, and things!"

"And don't forget the most important one—*sounds!*" Flame added. "I used to be scared of horns and sirens until Fireman James showed me the fire engine and let me discover it was nothing to be afraid of."

Fireman James was ready to get started on their park adventure. "Let's take Bear for a walk around the park and introduce him to *all kinds* of wonderful things!"

As the gang walked around the park, they encountered many new things. First they passed large trees and bushes, then two skateboarders passed by— *Whoosh!* Then, three bicyclist *zoomed* close by. They even slowed down to carefully pass a man walking with his cane. Bear had many different reactions.

When they passed a group of people playing soccer ball, he was both curious and apprehensive.

Then, they reached the end of their adventure at the park. Fireman James said, "Well, my newest E.P.T.'s, we've been on quite an adventure. What do you say we all enjoy some ice cream!"

Noah and Niki were thrilled, "Wow, that sounds great!" they both exclaimed.

POOF!

The group magically arrived at the ice cream parlor.

As Fireman James handed Noah and Niki their ice cream cones he said, "When you're training Bear you must always reward *good* behavior, just like I am rewarding you two for being such great E.P.T. Trainees!"

Niki and Noah thanked Fireman James for the yummy ice cream and for all the training tips.

Just as she was finishing the last of her cone Niki announced, "You were right Fireman James, puppy training sure is fun!"

Noah added, "I can't wait to start training Bear to become our own 'Super Dog!'"

Flame smiled happily at Fireman James. "Yup, I think they've got it."

"Ruff! Ruff!" added Bear.

Flame translated Bear's barks. "The 'little dude' says he can't wait to become a 'Super Dog,' but he needs a 'super nap' first!"

Fireman James knew the kids had the right amount of information to get started with their puppy training.

"Well, it's time to go kids. We've all had an incredibly big day, and it's time for Bear to take his nap," he said.

It was decided that they were all tired and it was time to take a rest as the gang was leaving the ice cream parlor.

POOF!

"Here we are!" says Fireman James.

Niki and Noah were both so grateful they met Fireman James and his wonderful sidekick, Flame. As she shook his hand Niki said, "Gosh! Thanks for the wonderful adventure Fireman James!"

Noah petted Flame on the head. "Thanks Flame—You're one cool dog, but there's one thing that you're missing," said Noah.

"What's that?" asked Flame.

Noah handed Flame his baseball cap. "A cool hat just like mine," said Noah. Then added, "But you have to wear it backwards to be really cool like me!"

"Awesome!" shouted Flame. "You guys have been totally cool."

Fireman James congratulated the kids. "You two did a great job today!"

"You honored your **E.P.T.** pledge by being **Prepared**, having **Patience**, and having **P-Fun**! So, it's my honor to award you both with your own **E.P.T.** badges!"

Fireman James handed the excited children their shiny new E.P.T. badges.

Noah and Niki said in unison, "Yeah! We did it!"

Flame patted Bear on the head. "Have fun with Bear," he said to the children. "The first year of his life is a magical time."

Fireman James addressed his new trainees. "Remember your training kids, Bear is counting on you!"

Fireman James and Flame got into the Magical Fire Engine on their way to another exciting adventure. "So long kids!" they shouted as Noah and Niki waived goodbye.

Fireman James' E.P.T. Training Tips

E.P.T.
OFFICIAL EXPERT PUPPY TRAINER

F.A.Q's

Q: What is the "Tug-And-A-No" technique?

A: The "Tug-And-A-No" technique is a moderate tug on your dog's leash while attached to their collar. At the same time you want to give a stern command of "NO!"

Q: What is a "Quiet Five?"

A: The "Quiet Five" is when you turn and ignore your puppy and count to five. This is used together with the "Tug-And-A-No" technique, This is used immediately after you have given your puppy a "Tug-And-A-No."

Potty Training

Never leave your puppy unattended in an area where you do not want him or her to have a potty accident. Your puppy should always be one of three places.

1. With you.
2. In their crate.
3. In their own dog run.

These rules should be continued until your puppy is potty trained.

Note: This may take many months, longer than most people think!

Jumping

Puppies tend to jump because people have shown their puppy affection as they jumped up. This most likely started before you ever met your puppy. But now your puppy is probably confused. They don't realize that leaping and jumping has now become a problem since they have grown bigger and stronger. You can handle this by giving your puppy a "Tug-And-A-No" and a "Quiet Five" whenever your puppy jumps up on anyone.

Mouthing

This is when your puppy chews on you. The reason he does this is to show you he thinks he is in charge of you. You need to give him a "Tug-And-A-No" and a "Quiet Five" immediately when he does this.

Chewing On Objects

There are too many different reasons to list as to why dogs chew on objects. The best way to handle this is to give the puppy a "Tug-And-A-No" while he is in the act of chewing, then replace the object of what he is chewing upon with one of his toys.

My inspiration for writing this book.

To the parents:

First and foremost, I believe family is the most important thing in the world. When adding a new puppy into your family it should be an exciting and wonderful experience. The day you bring your puppy home, it will be a moment you will never forget. This relationship will start with so much love and enthusiasm, but, unfortunately a well intended family will quickly become overwhelmed with the energy and vivaciousness of their new addition.

Their relationship with the new puppy starts to quickly spiral downhill. This is where I come in. For many years families have welcomed me into their homes with the desire for me to give them the knowledge they need to raise a happy, well-adjusted puppy.

I have found the biggest culprit of frustration a family will have experienced with a new puppy, is the simple lack of understanding of how the other thinks. With many years of my personal experience, it has been easy to get a clear message through to the adults and their respective puppies, but the confusion and follow through in the children is a different story. There's a lot about raising a puppy that young kids have a hard time understanding.

This is why I was inspired to write a series of educational guide books geared specifically for children, under the guidance of their parents, to understand basic training tips. I hope this first book, "I Have a New Puppy! Now What?," will help parents teach their children how to train their new puppy and raise them to be a trusted companion in their lives for many years to come.

To the kids—this book was written for you!

I know how much you love your new puppy, but sometimes your puppy can be a little hard to handle. Over the years I have been able spend time with lots of kids just like you.

They all tell me how much they love their new puppy, but they don't like how their puppies jump, mouth and chew on all their toys. So I wrote this training book, "I Have a New Puppy! Now What?" just for you!

I hope when you've finished reading this book, you will know how to teach your puppy to become your best friend, and remember—have FUN!